D1826427

AUTUMN PIANO
and
other poems

AUTUMN PIANO

and other poems

by

Penelope Shuttle

SELECTED BY TREVOR KNEALE, EDITOR, RONDO POETRY PAMPHLETS

— Abigail,

love from

Penny   July 74

Rondo Publications Limited
Liverpool

Published 1974 by
Rondo Publications Ltd., 10 Pall Mall,
Liverpool L3 6HJ

Copyright © 1974 Penelope Shuttle

ISBN 085619 007 1

Printed in Great Britain by The Acorn Press, Liverpool

FOR PETER

Acknowledgements
Meridian for "Dandelion Field",
Oasis for "Autumn Piano" and "Against Wives",
Cornish Review for "Yellow Chairs"
Samphire for "Granite Valentine"

CONTENTS

GIRLS AND THE RAIN

Between one sentence
and the next,
between one poem
and its sister,
my room has grown dark
It's nearly noon
but the sky is blueblack,
a splashboard for the rain
that is at last falling,
healing the wounds of girls
who are rescued by the rain
from a sad deformed morning

Waiting for rain,
my body was awkward
as the dusty cluttered furniture
and my empty purse
gaped open on the table

For me
and for the seaside girls like me,
the rainstorm
with its drops bevelling the windows,
the stammer and hiss of hail,
the revelation of the weather's veil,
the underside of the sky soaking
and clinging to the trees:
this is what we need

Dark icy tears fall from the sky
God, like a pale park-keeper, weeps for us,
tears tasting of piano-keyboards

And we are happier in our dark houses,
we draw our chairs close to the window
and peer through the glass at ourselves
seen as cloud-women
weeping ourselves clean

We dance in the last of the drizzle

AUTUMN PIANO

From my neighbour's parlour
I hear the echo
of an old self-playing piano:
cambric ghost of the ivories . . .

Angels annoyingly real
doodle with clouds
above the estuary

Careful reading of the scriptures
has given these angels the smiles of clowns

I carry a small basket of fruit
into my parlour
I knock my knuckles against the wooden table
and smile at the overnight dream

The basket is on the wooden table
Twilight turns the sky down,
dark, alert as a timpanist,
a blurred embryo for a moon

I stand at the window
The angels have gone from the estuary
and the uncelebrated waters
tug loneliness clumsily up the beaches

Adam's first wife plants lilies
in my garden
She smiles, her hands earthy,
and waves to me
from the other side of the dusky glass

I watch her walk
down to the beach,
her scarlet shawl wrapped around
her powerful shoulders

At the water's edge, she waits:
She waits for a humorous man
descended from clowns and angels
He will lead her home through the waxing shadows

I draw the curtain
My neighbour's pianola
blunders through a dance
made of the rhythms of consolation
then is silent

I miss the muslin refrain
as I watch the shadows from my lamp
twitch, oldest wounds

DANDELION FIELD

Old flowers grow on old walls
All moons are old, the skies they adjust
like shawls are old

Alphabets are old,
full of interchangeable beauties,
sadness of deceptions,
anguish of webs,
rag-dolls and picadors, uninterrupted lovers,
old divinities wallpapering the afternoon,
words like millinery adrift on an old sea

The sly anteater robbing a white ants' nest
is old
and the child turning the brightly-coloured page
of his first book is old

All the secret boxes have been opened
The women have done their work
All is old,
the miniature nipple growing on the tongue,
the odours of the blood bank,
the ornaments of Paphos,
the candles from the supermarket,
the off-white night-gown

Oldest of all, the clocks, the mirrors, the flames

There will be no more excursions into the mirrors
I have seen the mirrors grow old

The raw flame of the candle burns in my skull
I cannot blow it out

The clocks run the day
The night can only be admitted by clocks
Clocks have the password

Clocks unnerve me
I will not believe in their matchboxes, their salty trinkets
I tell time by watching the yellow field
Old parachutes land me safely in the dandelion patch
I puff the flower-head in the air
Fragments of the clock float back into my face

Here is the key to the smaller birds, to the thin grasses.

YELLOW CHAIRS

The chairs are yellow
The flowers in the yellow vase
are red
and their redness vexes the woman
wearing a blue dress
She believes this room is as unnatural
as a shop selling toys

She sits upon one of the two
yellow chairs
and she cannot move
out of the alphabet prison in which she has spent
her long unhappy day

The alphabet prison is the world's
sweet and viscous mouth
made of men's names and children's names
and official papers, lists fit only
for chimpanzees to memorise
Addresses of madmen
and jokes and appointments and quarrels:
a septicaemic language

But as she sits on her yellow chair
she thinks of the old photographs in the album,
the legend of the miracle-making heart,
the sheaves of night:
and the antidote flows through her body

She sits on a yellow tree
The red flowers open, stretch
and are beautiful in all mirrors
The woman smiles, the imbecilities fade

She is a simian woman
She is exhausted,
she cannot lean out of the window
to change the weather

She rises from her yellow chair
She opens the door of the garden
which is yellow with leaves
and the last of the fine crabbed sunlight

The day of tasks and apparitions
cannot meddle with her garden
The woman stands in her garden
and sees a pastoral country
She feels the betrothal of a green calendar
Her body goes through the garden with butterfly strokes

She sits on her yellow chair
beneath the new moon tree
until the leaves at her feet are amulets

GRANITE VALENTINE
for Peter

We are sheltered
We are in our granite tent
pitched two hundred years ago
and still baffling the winters
Against the night windows
Cornish snow is guzzling the wind
The snowflakes melt,
the lawns are hot-blooded here,
The wind butts at the doors,
whines along the cobweb passages

I sit by the fire,
on my lap is the book
you gave me this morning
"Granite Crosses of West Cornwall"

I open the book and read
"an ancient cross in the middle
of a field at Wicca"

This is the first Valentine
I've written
It came out of the gusty guesswork
of the spring
and commemorates one day
in our interwoven calendar

THE DEATH OF THE HYACINTH

One: The Candle

The yellow flame of the yellow candle
whirligigs out the end
of its life, the week of the candle is over

If the candle had a voice, I'd hear it croak
its offhand ending, the candle's last
unanswered question with its odour of hubbub

It is morning
The sky is colourless, after the manner
of a Cornish winter, clouds unploughed,
the fields rucked with seamist

In my winter room, I am searching
for the voice I had yesterday,
for the colour of my signature that turned
all the books into bibles,
made all doors thresholds leading
into the headquarters of the heart,
that region where I move touching leaves and serpents,
the small zoo of my opulence

Today, I am left outside
My books are books of interruption
The doors are locked
The weather says, you have asked for the last time

Today, I am burning down with my candle
My thoughts are ashy, my gestures clogged
as from the folds and gutterings of wax
I look at the calendar and turn the pages,
hurrying from January to March, from July to September,
on to the next snowflake, the next orchard

Two: The Moons

The moons are worked out for each month,
their dates are given, there is no mistake
The New and the Full, all the moons wait,
behind the sky: the haughty pearl moons,
the weak-minded moons, the fiery moons,
the doubtful bloodless moons

They smell of candles, these moons,
I see all the moons burning in the candle's saucer,
I burn with the moons,
my lazy skin burns, cannot shut out the fire,
my palms, breasts, my lips
are devouring all moons and all candles,
the octaves and loopholes of the heat are in me

I over-reach, I sob, I am begrimed
I want to grasp the monthly-minnow,
the shadow-membrane of me
Burrowing through the glass, I force myself
across a threshold,
tasting a blight like sour milk in my mouth

The colours are mere glimmers,
the flowers are annoyed and begin to die,
the little girl swabs the dead beast with hair,
this is not yesterday's room of good places
But I have travelled part of the way,
past the secret agents of the lavender
I cannot disown today's room, both rooms are mine

Today is a day run to seed
but I have hopped and limped and scrambled
to get here, to the borders of myself
This history tells of my attempt to see
what I am doing in this new year,
inside the pages of another calendar

Three: The Hyacinth

The white hyacinth that I kept for months
in a dark cupboard under the stairs
has died
Last week I brought the protected flower
out into the light, to let it bloom,
but it has died,
its bells are bedraggled, turning brown,
some flower-sickness is branching through it

Perhaps I should not have chosen
the white hyacinth, should have chosen the red

Perhaps I am clinging to an old year's habits,
performing old tasks, repeating the ceremonies,
and I've become unable to grow new vulnerable plants

The betrothal of candle and flower
I dreamt of
will not happen
One is dead
The other burnt out

Something else will happen,
another kind of marriage,
some new thing without bitterness,
which I will record and which will change me,
send me on new journeys
amid the web-worlds of the beckoning room

AGAINST WIVES

Opal autumn moon:
the housewives hate you
Your reincarnation is too real
for the married ladies
who sing phoney lullabies

Colours of deadlock dye the dresses
of the wives
to dark chevron shades
Their cartwheel hearts smell of scent
as they dance their men along
the paths of each herb garden

The smiles of the wives
are like a series of shallow waterfalls

But moon,
tasting like a deer's sweetbread,
tasting like pearly ink,
they don't want anything
to do with you,
the married ladies in their clean moonless rooms

The married ladies
have their Infantas
and Heirs to think of . . .
Hostages in perambulators . . .

New moon,
new arrival:
no welcome: the wives are walking in their apartments,
and can only scowl at the calm crescent knifing the window dark

The wives smile at one another like glass-makers,
they light candles in their own honour,
clutching the green jewels of their alimony . . .

Wives don't need moons
Lazy afternoons of sun burn their skins
brown as money
Sun needs no deciphering
and toughens lies and defections for winter

THE DEFEAT OF THE TROLLS
for Peter

Only one candle unmasks
the room
and the reconnoitres of the room
are dependent on the candle flame

The pastoral map
on the wall absorbs the land-locked
light
Megalithic ghosts dart
across the doorway, wedging into the light

There was danger today
heaving upwards with the redolence of gun-barrels
and horse-sweat
Tonight I draft my poems in red ink
No other colour can describe
the day's forfeits,
decipher the stale stories of the invaders

My book calls 'dittany' the candle plant
I love candle-light
Candles cause nights and dark mornings
to become deckled,
with edges uncut,
no doors closed

Fear fetched down from the old places
exhausted me today,
glowering through the outbursts of love
When I woke, the day smelt like the stage
of an ancient theatre

In the day, there were veiled colours
tamping the waters
There was a wintry tree full of brown birds
with beaks the colour of sawdust

There was a sea composed of grey feathers
I saw these mitigating things
I crunched the beauties up

But the apparel I wore
was wrinkled by my bad thoughts,
the clothes curdled on my flesh,
the fabrics were replete with cold,
patches of iron were nailed to my skirt

All day, bitter clowns spoke through my mouth

Until this evening
when we laid aside our old clothes,
our frightened thoughts,
and embraced

and bridges rippled snakily between us
in the infallible dance of lovers,
the webby consummation,
all the fragments frolicking together

Rising in the darkness,
we are the mended ruffians
Our smiles are no longer retarded

In your room, you read the magical book
In the next room, I light this candle,
zodiacing the room with cornish colours,
to celebrate the vanquishing
of the murky rabble,
the trolls who tried to catch our breath

PENELOPE SHUTTLE was born in 1947, and was educated at a private preparatory school and then at a secondary modern girls' school. She began writing seriously at the age of fourteen, and has been publishing poems in magazines since then. She completed her first novel at the age of seventeen, and by that time writing had become a pivotal passion, her life-style. She had taken a secretarial course at school and for several years worked as a "temporary secretary" in the Greater London area. In 1969, she moved from her parents' home in Middlesex to a cottage in Somerset, having always acknowledged an affinity with the West Country, and in early 1970, moved further West into Cornwall, where she has lived ever since, devoting all her time to writing. Other interests besides writing include: pre-history, archaeology, the visiting of the megalithic remains and earth-works of the West Country, walking, flower-pressing, Wicca, listening to all kinds of music, Tantra Yoga and beach-combing.

BIBLIOGRAPHY:
An Excusable Vengeance (New Writers 6).
Calder & Boyars, London, 1967.
Nostalgia Neurosis & Other Poems.
Aylesford Review Poets: 2 Saint Albert's Press, Aylesford, 1968.
All the Usual Hours of Sleeping.
Calder & Boyars, London, 1969.
Branch – poem-broadsheet.
The Sceptre Press, Rushden, 1971.
Jesusa – a poem-novel.
The Granite Press, Cornwall, 1972.
The Hermaphrodite Album. Poems with Peter Redgrove.
Fuller D'Arch Smith, London, April 1973.
Wailing Monkey Embracing a Tree. A novel.
Calder & Boyars, London, Autumn 1973.